LIVING IN THE
DAZE
OF DECEPTION

WORKBOOK

JACK HIBBS

HARVEST HOUSE PUBLISHERS
EUGENE, OREGON

Cover design by Faceout Studio

Cover images (c) tomertu, Igor Vitkovskiy, Golubovy / Shutterstock

Interior design by KUHN Design Group

For bulk, special sales, or ministry purchases, please call 1-800-547-8979. Email: CustomerService@hhpbooks.com

This logo is a federally registered trademark of the Hawkins Children's LLC. Harvest House Publishers, Inc., is the exclusive licensee of this trademark.

Living in the Daze of Deception Workbook
Copyright © 2024 by Jack Hibbs
Published by Harvest House Publishers
Eugene, Oregon 97408
www.harvesthousepublishers.com

ISBN 978-0-7369-9007-3 (pbk)
ISBN 978-0-7369-9008-0 (eBook)

Printed in the United States of America

24 25 26 27 28 29 30 31 32 / BP / 10 9 8 7 6 5 4 3 2 1

CONTENTS

PART 1

RECOGNIZING THE MANY KINDS OF DECEPTION

THE DAZE OF GLOBAL DECEPTION

T he thicker fog gets, the more dangerous it becomes. The same is true about deception. The more that deception abounds, the greater the need for us to exercise discernment in our everyday living.

Scripture tells us that as we approach earth's last days, deception will worsen. We are surrounded by hazards that are difficult to see. And the only way to safely navigate our way through the daze of deception is to walk in the light that God's Word provides. Though the Bible was written 2,000 years ago, it is filled with wisdom that addresses the crises we face today. The psalmist's declaration, "Your word is a lamp to my feet and a light to my path" is still true as ever (Psalm 119:105).

The Merriam-Webster Dictionary defines deception as "the act of causing someone to accept as true or valid what is false or invalid."* The reason deception is so tricky to avoid is that it masquerades as truth. Those who peddle lies present their narratives as truths with the intent to persuade and convince. And one of the most effective ways they do that is to shroud falsehood with some element of truth. It's that little bit of truth that is used to bait people into swallowing a lie.

The very definition of deception should tell us it is hard to recognize, which is why we need to exercise so much caution.

Jesus warned this would happen as our world draws closer to the last days. When the disciples asked the Lord about the signs of His future return, what were His very first words? "Take heed that no one deceives you" (Matthew 24:4).

We dare not take our Lord's exhortation lightly. That's because deception can cause us to stray from God's path—and His light. It can leave us stumbling in the darkness, vulnerable to errors that can cause great harm to us.

GROWING IN DISCERNMENT

As you answer the following questions, you'll want to have your Bible in hand, as well as your copy of the book *Living in the Daze of Deception*.

---

* Merriam Webster, s.v. "deception," https://www.merriam-webster.com/dictionary/deception.

1. What are two or three examples of deception you've noticed in recent weeks?

2. Oftentimes a falsehood is shrouded with enough truth to make it seem believable. Give one example of how you've seen this happen before.

3. Can you think of a time when you heard or read something, but you weren't sure it was true? When you are uncertain about a claim or a statement, what do you think is the best way to respond, and why?

4. On page 17 of *Living in the Daze of Deception*, we read about the classic legend of the Trojan horse. What trickery was carried out in this tale?

5. In the account about the Trojan horse, it was the packaging (the wooden horse) that hid the danger within (the Greek soldiers). The strategy of using deceptive packaging is not new. Read the following passages. In each case, identify the attractive package presented by the one doing the deceiving:

   a. Genesis 3:1-7—

b. Matthew 4:8-11—

c. Revelation 13:11-13—

6. Oftentimes a falsehood is successful only because the person who is spreading it is able to control the flow of information. Share about a time when you've seen this happen.

7. When it comes to watching out for those who control the flow of information for the purpose of deception, what wisdom do we find in Proverbs 18:17?

8. What scripture applies to every Christian in these last days, and why? (See page 18 of *Living in the Daze of Deception.*)

9. What criticism did Jesus give to the religious leaders of His day in Matthew 16:2-3, and why? (See page 19.)

10. According to 1 Timothy 3:2-4, what attitudes and behaviors can we expect from people in the last days?

11. What does 2 Timothy 4:3-4 warn that people will turn away from? What will they pursue instead?

12. On pages 21 to 29 of *Living in the Daze of Deception*, we learn that the events of the last days have been designed

   • to validate God

   • to validate the Bible

   • to validate Jesus Christ

   • to validate the Messiah's identity

   • to get our attention

On the next page, let's take a closer look at these purposes.

a. To Validate God

What absolute truths does God proclaim about Himself in Isaiah 46:9-10 and Isaiah 45:21-22?

b. To Validate the Bible

According to 2 Peter 1:19, why can we trust God's Word? (See page 23.)

c. To Validate Jesus Christ

What did Jesus mean when He said, "Now I tell you before it comes, that when it does come to pass, you may believe that I am He" (John 13:19)? What is the significance of "I AM" here? (See page 25.)

d. To Validate the Messiah's Identity

How do Micah 5:2, paired with Matthew 2:4-6, and Psalm 40:6-8, paired with Hebrews 10:5-10, validate Jesus as the Messiah? (See pages 26-28.)

e. To Get Our Attention

As the world around us gets worse, what should we be doing, according to Hebrews 10:23-25? (See page 29.)

13. When Jesus spoke about the last days, He said, "See that you are not troubled" (Matthew 24:6). Why should we not be troubled, according to John 16:33? (See pages 30-31.)

SEEKING CLARITY

"When it comes to spiritual realities, there's only one way to know the truth. That, of course, is the Bible—the inerrant, perfect, never-changing Word of God. When the church—the ground and pillar of all truth—proclaims the whole counsel of God from the Bible, deception will not and cannot take hold."

Living in the Daze of Deception, page 21

14. What benefits can we derive from the Bible, according to the following passages?

a. Psalm 1:2-4—

b. Psalm 19:7-11—

c. Psalm 119:11—

d. 2 Timothy 3:16-17—

15. Read Romans 12:2. What types of influences can cause us to become conformed to this world? And why does it make sense that constant exposure to Scripture helps to transform and renew our mind?

LIVING WISELY

16. Colossians 3:16 urges us to "let the word of Christ dwell in [us] richly."

a. What are some practical ways we can actively fill our minds and hearts with the Word?

b. Where do you see room for improvement when it comes to filling yourself with the truths of Scripture?

PRAYING DILIGENTLY

Pray "search me, O God, and know my heart" (Psalm 139:23). Ask the Lord to reveal to you any weaknesses in your life that make you vulnerable to deception. Commit yourself to being firmly rooted in God's Word so that you possess the discernment that will help you to avoid deception.

DAZED BY SPIRITUAL DECEIVERS

Typically when we think about threats faced by the church today, our first thoughts go to the opposition we encounter from an unbelieving world. We point to the constant pressure we face from contemporary culture—pressure that urges us to compromise God's truth and our convictions.

But the greater threat we face as Christians comes from inside the church, which we normally wouldn't expect. This has been true from the time the church was first born. Through the ages, spiritual deceivers have "crept in unnoticed," as Jude 4 says, and spread their false teachings inside the church.

Jesus knew how serious a problem this would be. Early in His ministry, He warned, "Beware of false prophets, who come to you in sheep's clothing, but inwardly they are ravenous wolves" (Matthew 7:15). Before the apostle Paul left from the church at Ephesus, he exhorted the leaders there, saying, "I know this, that after my departure savage wolves will come in among you, not sparing the flock" (Acts 20:29).

Similar alerts appear all throughout the New Testament. The problem was so serious that only a short time after Paul delivered the true gospel to the church at Galatia, some people were already "turning away…to a different gospel." They had been misled by teachers who "want to pervert the gospel of Christ" (Galatians 1:6-7). Spiritual deceivers had wasted no time infiltrating the church, spreading their lies and pulling people away from the truth.

Before we get to the final book of the Bible, we find the short epistle of Jude. The entire letter is a fierce condemnation of false teachers who were spreading error and corruption within the church.

Spiritual deception has always been a challenge for the church, which is why we can never let down our guard. These deceivers are able to cause great harm because they profess Christ and they appear to be trustworthy teachers when, in reality, they aren't.

What do we need to know so we can protect ourselves?

GROWING IN DISCERNMENT

As you answer the following questions, you'll want to have your Bible in hand, as well as your copy of the book *Living in the Daze of Deception*.

1. Why does it make sense that deceivers inside the church can be more dangerous than enemies outside the church?

2. In today's Christian circles, what are some examples of incorrect teaching that you are aware of?

3. What claims do we see false teachers make to Jesus in Matthew 7:22? How does Jesus respond to them in verse 23?

4. In Matthew chapter 23, when Jesus condemned the religious leaders of His day, what accusation(s) did He bring against them in...

   a. verse 4?

   b. verse 5?

c. verses 6 and 7?

d. verse 13?

e. verse 14?

f. verse 23?

g. verses 27-28?

5. On page 35 of *Living in the Daze of Deception*, we read that "even in religious circles, appearances can be misleading." In Matthew 7:16-20, what test does Jesus say we should apply to spiritual teachers?

6. Read 2 Peter 2:1-2. What does Peter condemn false teachers for?

What does Peter say about these destructive influencers in verses 18 and 19?

7. Another way to spot spiritual deceivers is to observe what they love. Read 2 Timothy 3:1-5, then answer the following:

a. What are some of the characteristics of those who are lovers of self? (See pages 38-39.)

b. What perspective do those who love money have about ministry, according to 1 Timothy 6:5?

(1) And what does their love of money lead to, according to 1 Timothy 6:10?

(2) In contrast, what is true about those who do *not* have a love for money, according to 1 Timothy 6:8?

c. Second Timothy 3:4 says false teachers are "lovers of pleasure rather than lovers of God."

(1) What would you expect to see from someone who is a lover of pleasure?

(2) What would you expect to see from someone who is a lover of God?

8. On page 42 of *Living in the Daze of Deception*, we read that false teachers "are always guilty of this one act: undermining the deity of Jesus Christ." In contrast, Scripture makes it clear Jesus is God. How do the following passages affirm Christ's deity?

a. John 1:1, 14—

b. John 10:30—

    c. John 20:28—

    d. Colossians 1:15-20—

    e. Colossians 2:9—

9. Why do false teachers hate God's grace so much? (See page 44.)

10. Spiritual deceivers say that Christ's sacrifice on the cross isn't enough. They claim, "You still need to do all you can." But what does Scripture say, according to the following passages?

    a. Ephesians 2:8-9—

b. Titus 3:4-5—

c. Romans 11:6—

11. What did Jesus say about deceivers in John 10:1? In verses 8-10, what did Jesus say they do?

12. In Ephesians 4:14, Paul urged that we "no longer be children, tossed to and fro and carried about with every wind of doctrine, by the trickery of men."

a. What are the two antidotes to incorrect teaching, according to verse 15?

b. What does the teaching of sound doctrine do to the health of a church?

SEEKING CLARITY

"False teachers want to rob you of your liberty and freedom in Christ and replace it with a counterfeit gospel and false doctrines that will lead into bondage. Don't let that become your fate."

Living in the Daze of Deception, page 46

13. What exhortation are we given in 1 Thessalonians 5:21-22?

    What are some ways we can apply this exhortation?

14. According to 2 Timothy 4:3-4, why is it so easy for false teachers to attract followers?

15. Is there a difference between a false teacher and someone who unintentionally teaches an error? Explain.

16. In what ways would our response to a false teacher differ from our response to an otherwise trustworthy teacher who happens to teach a doctrine or principle incorrectly?

LIVING WISELY

17. Second Peter 2:10 reveals some of the fruit we can expect from spiritual deceivers: They will "walk according to the flesh in the lust of uncleanness and despise authority." More simply, they will be defiled and defiant. They will pursue filthy pleasures and reject God's authority over them.

    In contrast, according to the following passages, how does Scripture call true followers of Christ to live?

    a. Galatians 5:22-23—

    b. Colossians 3:12-17—

18. In 2 Peter 3:17-18, we read this: "Beware lest you also fall from your own steadfastness, being led away with the error of the wicked; but grow in the grace and knowledge of our Lord and Savior Jesus Christ."

    Notice that Peter points out how we can avoid error: "grow in the grace and knowledge of our Lord and Savior Jesus Christ." This calls for hungering and thirsting for Christ—for abiding in Him (John 15:4-5) and letting His word dwell richly in us (Colossians 3:16).

The closer you are to the Great Shepherd, the less likely you are to be deceived. What do you think a close walk with Christ looks like?

PRAYING DILIGENTLY

Ask the Lord to give you a greater love for Him and His Word so you can protect yourself against false teachings. Make it a priority to "test all things" (1 Thessalonians 5:21) so that you train yourself to exercise discernment at all times. When you lack the wisdom to tell the difference between truth and error, pray. "Ask of God, who gives to all liberally" (James 1:5), and He will guide you.

DAZED BY DECEPTIVE SPIRITS

First John chapter 4 opens with this firm plea from the apostle John: "Beloved, do not believe every spirit, but test the sprits, whether they are of God; because many false prophets have gone out into the world" (verse 1). The Greek tense that John used for the word "test" tells us this is an ongoing, never-ending activity for the believer. We can never rest from the task of separating truth from error.

We find a wonderful role model for us in Acts 17:11. There, we read about the Christians in Berea, who "received the word with all readiness, and searched the Scriptures daily to find out whether these things were so." They listened eagerly to what was taught by spiritual teachers, and they carefully compared it to God's Word to make sure it was true. They did this daily. In this way, they could tell truth from error.

The Bible is the one source we can trust to help us test everything we read and hear. We are to take man's word and measure it against God's Word, which is perfect and trustworthy.

The reason we must be so careful is because false teachers "secretly bring in destructive heresies" (2 Peter 2:1). The word "secretly" tells us they do their work subtly. The errors they proclaim are mixed with truth, making it more difficult to catch the falsehoods.

Notice that Satan went so far as to quote Scripture when he tempted Jesus. He hoped to trick the Lord and lure Him into sin. In the second of three temptations, the devil said, "If You are the Son of God, throw Yourself down. For it is written: 'He shall give His angels charge over you,' and, 'In their hands they shall bear you up, lest you dash your foot against stone'" (Matthew 4:6). Here, Satan quoted Psalm 91:11-12.

Jesus knew Satan was trying to manipulate Him. He recognized the evil intent hidden behind the truths the devil cited from the Bible. And the Lord answered, using Scripture: "It is written again, 'You shall not tempt the LORD your God'" (Matthew 4:7).

Satan will twist truths to achieve his ends, and spiritual deceivers will do the same. That's why it is so vital for us to "test the spirits, whether they are of God."

GROWING IN DISCERNMENT

As you answer the following questions, you'll want to have your Bible in hand, as well as your copy of the book *Living in the Daze of Deception*.

1. In *Living in the Daze of Deception*, we read, "Wherever you find a work of God and the Holy Spirit having free reign to do as they will, you will find Satan, your enemy, at work." Why do you think Satan is so eager to do damage to the church? Try to come up with at least three reasons:

    a. Reason 1:

    b. Reason 2:

    c. Reason 3:

2. The admonishments to test the spirits and search the Scriptures reveal that it's good to ask questions of spiritual teachers. When teachers refuse to answer, what should we do? (See page 51 in *Living in the Daze of Deception*.)

3. What are some popular misconceptions about God or Christianity that you have noticed on the internet, social media, or television? Try to list at least three.

   a. Misconception 1:

   b. Misconception 2:

   c. Misconception 3:

4. What kind of damage can be caused by each of the misconceptions you listed above?

   a. Destructive result(s) 1:

   b. Destructive result(s) 2:

c. Destructive result(s) 3:

5. Two areas in which there is enormous confusion today are (1) how to get to heaven, and (2) the existence of hell. If you don't know the answers to the questions below, do the necessary research to find out. For help, you can use a Bible dictionary and a concordance.

   a. What Scripture passages would you use to correct someone who claims there are many ways to heaven?

   b. What Bible verses would you share with someone who doesn't believe hell is real or a place of eternal punishment?

6. According to 2 Corinthians 11:13, what do false apostles and deceitful workers transform themselves into?

7. But no matter how false teachers disguise themselves, what will always be true about them, according to Matthew 7:16-20?

8. On page 55 of *Living in the Daze of Deception*, we read, "Part of the devil's craftiness is lulling you into believing you are doing just fine while he is quietly at work. He does his best to weave lies into and around your heart, mind, spirit, and soul, to the point where he has you bound and captive."

When we are concerned about demonically driven deception, what do the following Bible verses help us to remember?

a. 1 John 4:4—

b. 2 Timothy 1:7—

9. According to 1 Thessalonians 5:21, how many things are we to test? (See page 55.)

10. One tactic deceivers use is to manipulate and redefine words.

a. What are a couple examples of how you've seen this done in the secular world?

b. What are a couple examples of how you've seen this done in the religious realm?

11. John 7:24 says, "Do not judge according to appearance, but judge with righteous judgment." What does this mean? (See page 59.)

12. When it comes to arriving at correct conclusions, who is our helper, according to John 14:16-17?

13. As we look to the Bible to stay centered on God's truth, what two resources can we use to help us better understand it? (See page 61.)

14. When it comes to seeking God's guidance, how can fasting be helpful? (See pages 61-62.)

15. What is the intent of prayer? (See page 62.)

16. What does it mean to "pray without ceasing" (1 Thessalonians 5:17)? (See page 62.)

SEEKING CLARITY

> "The more familiar you are with the whole counsel of God, the more quickly truth becomes visible. Scripture shows us the heart and mind—the very will—of God. It is the guide for what to look for, how to look, and what to do when you see it. When armed this way, you are less likely to stumble."
>
> *Living in the Daze of Deception*, page 61

17. Notice that the statement above doesn't say, "The more you *read* the whole counsel of God," but rather, "The more *familiar* you are with the whole counsel of God." How is becoming *familiar* with Scripture different from merely *reading* it?

18. What are some ways you can go from simply reading to becoming familiar with God's Word, and let it permeate your mind and heart to the point of true change?

LIVING WISELY

19. Proverbs 3:5-6 offers these words of wisdom to us:

    Trust in the LORD with all your heart,
    And lean not on your own understanding.
    In all your ways acknowledge Him,
    And He shall direct your paths.

    a. How much are we to trust the Lord?

b. Why do you think we're told not to lean on our own understanding?

c. To what extent are we to acknowledge the Lord—that is, look to Him, hear Him, revere Him, and agree with Him?

d. When we yield ourselves completely to the Lord, what will He do?

PRAYING DILIGENTLY

God promises wisdom to those who ask for it (James 1:5). And we're told to "test all things"—*all!* (1 Thessalonians 5:21). Cultivate a habit of asking God to help you evaluate everything you read and hear. Ask yourself, "Do these thoughts, beliefs, and ideas align with God and His Word, or not?" The more proactive you are in doing this, the less likely you are to stumble or be led astray.

DAZED BY DOCTRINES OF DEMONS

In every matter pertaining to life, we can either trust God, or Satan. We can either heed the truth or listen to lies. We can submit to the authority of the right teacher or succumb to the wrong one.

In Psalm 119:160, we read that "the sum of [God's] word is truth." Jesus said the same in John 17:17, declaring that God's "word is truth." In contrast, John 8:44 says the devil "is a liar and the father of it."

God is the source of all truth, and Satan is the source of all lies.

Doctrines are principles, teachings, or instructions that are considered authoritative. With that in mind, it makes sense that good doctrines come from God and are trustworthy, and bad doctrines come from Satan and are harmful. So when we speak of doctrines of demons, we are referring to deceptions and lies.

One way to understand all this is to recognize that a lie distorts what is true. A lie is inaccurate and misleading. Whereas truth will lead us to light and life, lies will lead us into darkness and despair. Speaking in terms of a person's choice to follow or reject Christ, we can say that the doctrines a person chooses to follow will mean the difference between life and death.

This should give us some idea of how dangerous the doctrines of demons are. As Jesus said, "thieves and robbers"—that is, Satan, demons, and false teachers—"come...to steal, and to kill, and to destroy" (John 10:8, 10). Those who lie do not have our best interests in mind. Their intent is to appeal to our fleshly desires, which lead to discontent rather than fulfillment. We know all too well that when we give in to temptation and sin, despair and guilt become our companions. And there's a detrimental impact on our relationship with God.

God seeks our good, and Satan seeks our destruction. Good doctrines are meant to build us up, and bad doctrines are meant to tear us down. That's how devastating doctrines of demons can be.

How can we identify whether ideas and beliefs are of God, or of demons?

GROWING IN DISCERNMENT

As you answer the following questions, you'll want to have your Bible in hand, as well as your copy of the book *Living in the Daze of Deception*.

1. What question should we ask when we see a person engaged in an activity or living in a way that appeals to us? (See page 66 of *Living in the Daze of Deception*.)

2. What has been Satan's goal since the garden of Eden? (See pages 66-67.)

3. In 2 Timothy 3:1, Paul wrote, "Know this, that in the last days perilous times will come." What does the word "perilous" mean here? (See page 67.)

4. Why do you think continual stress can make us more vulnerable to bad doctrines?

5. On page 68, we read, "An imperceptible shift has been taking place under the foundations and pillars upon which we once stood." Give at least two or three examples of cultural or ideological shifts that have occurred over the past several years.

6. In what ways have you noticed today's churches drifting loose from the foundational doctrines of the Bible?

7. What does progressivism's subversive doctrines do with God? (See page 70.)

8. What is the dark side of social media? (See page 71.)

9. How has social media become an effective tool for Satan? (See page 72.)

10. What are the two primary secular viewpoints on life? (See page 72.)

11. What do atheists fail to recognize? (See page 72.)

12. Why is perverting and redefining sexuality so important to Satan? (See page 73.)

13. When people give credence to the idea of alien or alternate life forms, what are they usually looking for a way out of? (See page 74.)

14. What does the account about New Zealand Air Flight 901 illustrate for us? (See page 75.)

15. What happens when we perceive God's judgments as being too harsh? (See page 77.)

16. What is greater than any force coming against us? (See page 79.)

17. In 1 John 4:1, when the apostle warned about testing the spirits, he called us "beloved." How great is God's love for us, according to Romans 8:38-39?

SEEKING CLARITY

"Believer, get alone with God, just you and Him. Read His love letter to you—the Bible. It's there that He will show you His character and His ways. His promises will become the love language that fortifies your soul. Then, when the devil offers alternatives, you'll have the strength and knowledge to resist."

Living in the Daze of Deception, page 80

18. Why does it make sense that God's promises—His reminders of His love for you— would motivate you to resist the lies of demons?

19. Charles Spurgeon said, "Love God, and you will not love false doctrine." Why do you think that as your love for God increases, your attraction to the world's lies will decrease?

LIVING WISELY

20. When it comes to living the Christian life, we have only two choices: to walk according to good doctrine, or to succumb to bad doctrine. Here's another way of looking at it: For us to live according to good doctrine is to show love for God. And to give ourselves over to Satan's lies is to demonstrate love for self.

    In the left column below, write what it looks like for a person to love God. In the right column, write what it looks like to love self.

    Characteristics of Love for God   **Characteristics of Love for Self**

    After you've finished your two lists, ask yourself:

    a. What do we gain from loving God and abiding by good doctrine?

    b. What do we lose when we love self and give in to bad doctrine?

21. What are we telling God when we choose to stay on course, submit to His authority, and anchor our lives to good doctrine?

PRAYING DILIGENTLY

As long as we live in bodies of flesh, we will find ourselves vulnerable to Satan's lies. As Paul said in Romans 7:15, "What I am doing, I do not understand. For what I will to do, that I do not practice; but what I hate, that I do." This speaks of the struggle between doing what is right and giving in to what is wrong. Take time now to pray and surrender yourself completely to God. Place yourself fully in His hands. Remember the abundance of ways He has shown His love for you. Keep in mind that a growing love for God diminishes your love for self. In these ways, you will fortify yourself against the doctrines of demons.

DAZED BY DECEPTIONS WITHIN THE CHURCH

What is God's purpose for the church? To shine the light of the gospel into a dark world lost in sin. Every Christian is an ambassador for Christ (2 Corinthians 5:20), and our job is to point people away from sin and toward God.

For this to happen, it is necessary for the church to distinguish itself from the world. People must see that we are different. We're called to live in a way that rejects worldly values and accepts the fact that, as Christians, we're at odds with the world's way of thinking. James 4:4 affirms this truth with this exhortation: "Do you not know that friendship with the world is enmity with God? Whoever therefore wants to be a friend of the world makes himself an enemy of God."

Jesus warned about the friction that is inevitable between the church and the world: "If the world hates you, know that it hated Me before it hated you. If you were of the world, the world would love its own. Yet because you are not of the world, but I chose you out of the world, therefore the world hates you" (John 15:18-19).

Why do the lost hate Christ? Jesus said, "The world...hates Me because I testify of it that its works are evil." And when we as Christians walk in Christ's footsteps, our words and lives will, by default, rebuke the world, leading it to hate us as well.

Yet now there are people in the church who say that for us to reach the lost, we must reinvent the gospel so it's more attractive. We must get the world to like us by being more winsome, setting aside our convictions and accepting people as they are.

The result? Instead of the church being an influence on the world, the world is influencing the church. Instead of the church changing the way the lost think, the lost are changing the way the church thinks. Instead of holding fast to truth, the church is embracing error.

Let's look at some of the ways this is happening, and learn what must be done to preserve God's purpose for the church.

GROWING IN DISCERNMENT

As you answer the following questions, you'll want to have your Bible in hand, as well as your copy of the book *Living in the Daze of Deception*.

1. What did the apostle Paul say about the gospel in Romans 1:16? (See page 82 of *Living in the Daze of Deception*.)

2. What is the difference between a backslider and an apostate? (See pages 82-83.)

3. How does Jude 12 describe pastors and teachers who marry secular ideologies to Scripture? (See page 83.)

4. On page 83 of *Living in the Daze of Deception*, we read this:

    Churches spend an enormous amount of time and effort conforming themselves to the whims of the day rather than the gospel. What they fail to realize is that God's Word does not need human help, power, nor intervention. The Lord never strives to be relevant to the culture.

    In what ways have you seen churches striving to be relevant with the culture? Why is it dangerous to do this?

5. What does the gospel call us to do about sin? In contrast, what do apostates do about sin? (See page 83.)

6. What happened to those who were in the church at Laodicea? (See pages 84-85.)

7. What have new ways of interpreting Scripture led to? (See page 85.)

8. What is the danger of failing to teach the Old Testament adequately? (See page 86 of *Living in the Daze of Deception*, and support your answer using Matthew 5:17-18 and 2 Timothy 3:16.)

9. What does replacement theology teach about Israel and the church? (See pages 87-88.)

10. What evidence do we see in Daniel 9:24-27 that God still has future plans for Israel? (See pages 88-90, and note what is said about the final seven-year period in the 70-weeks prophecy.)

11. If we say that God's past promises to Israel have been canceled, what can we logically say about the security of God's promises to us today?

12. What two landmark decisions in 1973 altered the way society views God's design for men and women? (See pages 90-91.)

13. What does Genesis 1:27-28 say is God's design for men and women, and how does this passage rebuke humanity's approval of abortion and same-sex relationships? (See page 91.)

14. How does society frequently portray men? (See pages 92-93.)

15. What does biblical masculinity look like? (See page 93.)

16. On page 94 of *Living in the Daze of Deception*, we read, "That God made men and women differently is not a comment on their value before Him—both are of equal worth." Why did God gift women in ways that men aren't, and vice versa? (See pages 94-95.)

17. What does Luke 12:35 urge us to do in these days when many have distorted or watered down God's Word?

SEEKING CLARITY

"Those who understand the times know that night is coming…God has purposefully placed you and me in this moment of history. Are you dressed for service? Are you prepared? Are you holding up your lamp so others can see what's going on around them?"

Living in the Daze of Deception, page 97

18. What exhortation are we given in Hebrews 12:1?

a. What types of sins can easily weigh us down? Why do you think we should be serious about avoiding even the seemingly "small" sins in life?

b. Hebrews 12:1 calls us to "run with endurance." What does this communicate to you?

19. What does Peter call us to do in 1 Peter 1:13?

a. How we use our minds will determine how well we run the race. Why do you think Matthew 22:37 urges us to "love the LORD your God...with *all* your mind"?

b. What do you think can happen when we allow the world's way of thinking to infiltrate our mind?

LIVING WISELY

20. Even the smallest amount of compromise can affect our witness to the world. It can diminish our impact as salt and light. That's why 1 Peter 1:15-16 urges, "He who called you is holy, you also be holy in all your conduct, because it is written, 'Be holy, for I am holy.'"

What do the following passages teach us about living an unhindered life—a life that influences the world, and not the other way around?

   a. Romans 12:1-2—

   b. Ephesians 2:10—

   c. Ephesians 5:8—

   d. Colossians 3:1-3, 12—

21. Holiness is more than simply putting off sin. What does Romans 8:29 say is God's goal in our lives?

22. What is at stake when we allow compromise to seep into our lives?

23. Why can we correctly say that to pursue holiness is to show God how much we love Him?

PRAYING DILIGENTLY

Ask the Lord to help you not be afraid of the world's criticism and hatred. Commit yourself to seeking to please God, and not those around you. Yield yourself as an instrument available for the Master's use, an instrument not impaired by compromise.

DAZED BY EASY BELIEVISM

The gospel is timeless. The remedy for sin has not changed. There is nothing a person can do to participate in their salvation. Only the sinless Lamb of God is able to cleanse us of our sins and bring us back into relationship with God. That's why He went to the cross. He paid a high price to break us free from the bondage of sin—He paid with His life.

An essential element of the gospel message is that every person is a sinner. As Romans 3:10-11 says, "There is none righteous, no, not one. There is none who understands; there is none who seeks after God." About a dozen verses later, we read, "All have sinned and fall short of the glory of God" (verse 23). That's *all*. No exceptions.

Sin is the problem, and Christ is the solution.

Yet we live in a day when speaking to people about sin is considered offensive and judgmental. In an effort to accommodate the culture and attract people to Jesus, there are some within the church who are softening the gospel. They are updating it and adapting it to the times. There is a reluctance to call people sinners. Instead, it is said that people are basically good. They mean well, and simply don't know better.

But what happens when sin isn't taken seriously? What happens when people don't realize how sin affects their standing before God, and how it determines their eternal destiny?

Without a right understanding of sin and the gospel, people won't realize their need for Christ or salvation. If we don't explain the penalty and consequences of sin, the lost won't see their need to turn away from it. And rather than view Jesus as a Savior, they're likely to view Him as a helper or friend who wants to make life easier for them. But that's not why Jesus came.

A gospel that is made easier for people to hear is a gospel that leaves people with wrong impressions of sin and the Savior. It puts people on the wrong path to a destiny they don't expect.

What is the gospel, and what is it not?

GROWING IN DISCERNMENT

As you answer the following questions, you'll want to have your Bible in hand, as well as your copy of the book *Living in the Daze of Deception*.

1. What do we learn from the parable of the tares in Matthew 13:24-30? (See page 101 of *Living in the Daze of Deception*.)

2. What was Jesus telling us in the parables of the mustard seed and the leaven? (See page 102.)

3. What is the modernized gospel based on, and what has it departed from? (See page 102.)

4. Give two or three examples of the felt needs churches are emphasizing today to attract people to Christ rather than proclaiming the gospel.

5. What is the danger of substituting the gospel with a felt-needs approach to reaching people? (See page 103.)

6. Why does it not make sense to present the gospel without bringing up sin?

7. What role is conviction meant to play when it comes to proclaiming the gospel? (See page 105.)

8. What does the Bible alone have the power to do, according to Hebrews 4:12? (See page 105.)

9. What is repentance, and why is it such an essential part of the gospel? (See pages 106-107.)

10. What does easy believism within the church produce, and what is the effect on people's lives? (See page 107.)

11. When we proclaim the gospel, is it possible to do so without mentioning the cross? Why?

12. What hard truths did Jesus teach in Matthew 16:24-26? (See page 110.)

13. What are some reasons we find ourselves ashamed of the gospel?

14. Is there such a thing as a no-cost, no-cross Christianity? Explain.

15. What is one of the most effective forms of evangelism? (See page 111.)

16. What does picking up the cross and following Jesus involve? Why is this a good thing? (See page 113.)

SEEKING CLARITY

> "The cross comes at a cost to your pride and self-will. God designed it that way. He uses the ugly and difficult things in our lives as instruments of growth toward Christlikeness, which, in turn, clearly display the gospel's transforming power."
>
> *Living in the Daze of Deception*, page 113

When we receive Christ as Savior, we cannot cling to our pride and self-will. Rather, we must humble ourselves before the Lord, confess our sin, repent (or turn away) from our sin, and place our faith in Christ as the one who can remove our sin because of what He did at the cross. In doing this, we yield ourselves completely to the Lord's authority—to His will.

17. What is the result of repentance, according to Acts 3:19?

18. What do Ephesians 2:8 and Titus 3:5 say about how we are saved?

19. Read 2 Corinthians 5:21. When Christ took our sins upon Himself, what did He make possible for us?

20. What does true salvation produce in a person, according to 2 Corinthians 5:17?

LIVING WISELY

21. So that you will never be guilty of presenting a gospel of easy believism, commit to remembering the following essentials of helping unbelievers to receive Christ as their Savior. Below each step, write out the words in the passages cited.

    Step 1: Realize that you are a sinner (read Romans 3:10-11, 23)—

Step 2: Recognize that Jesus Christ died on the cross for you (read Romans 5:8)—

Step 3: Repent of your sin and go the other way (read Acts 3:19)—

Step 4: Receive Jesus Christ into your life (read Romans 10:9-10)—

PRAYING DILIGENTLY

If you are already a believer, take time now to thank God for the tremendous sacrifice He made, through the death of His Son on the cross, so you could come back to Him. Pray also that you would never shy away from proclaiming the gospel clearly and directly. It's better to offend someone temporarily about their sinful state and point them to eternal life than it is to ignore their sin and leave them on the path to eternal condemnation.

DAZED BY THE DECEPTIVE CRY FOR UNITY

B elievers are called to unity with one another. One of the most powerful reminders of this is found in a prayer Jesus uttered to His heavenly Father. He prayed that we "all may be one…[so that] the world may believe that You sent Me" (John 17:21). Our unity can serve as a testimony that convinces the lost that they need Christ as their Savior because He can truly transform lives. Earlier, Jesus told His disciples, "By this all will know that you are my disciples, if you have love for one another" (John 13:35).

The apostle Paul admonished the Christians in Philippi with these words: "Fulfill my joy by being like-minded, having the same love, being of one accord, of one mind. Let nothing be done through selfish ambition or conceit, but in lowliness of mind let each esteem others better than himself" (Philippians 2:2-3). In other words, humility leads to unity.

From a *positional* standpoint, because of our salvation in Christ, all believers are united because we are part of the one body of Christ, and we share the same Holy Spirit (Ephesians 4:4). We also possess the same hope—we were "called to the one hope" (verse 5), and we have all been sealed with the same Spirit, which guarantees all of us the same eternal inheritance (Ephesians 1:13-14). We all follow one Lord, hold to the same faith, and are all baptized in Christ (Ephesians 4:5). And we all worship and submit to the same God (verse 6). In all these ways, we are one by virtue of what Christ has done for us or given to us.

From a *practical* standpoint, however, experiencing unity is more of a challenge. While it is necessary for all of us to agree on the core doctrines of the faith that truly make us Christians, we will vary in our opinions about some of the "gray areas" of the Christian life. Or we'll let divisions over worldly matters damage our spiritual unity. For one reason or another, we will disagree, and that can be detrimental to our oneness.

But there's a unity that's becoming popular that isn't really unity at all—it's known as ecumenical unity. In an effort to be in agreement with others who hold to different beliefs, there are some who sacrifice important biblical doctrines purely for the sake of "getting along" on other matters.

The result is a unity that is superficial and breaks easily, rather than a unity that is strong because it is deeply rooted in the foundational truths of the Christian faith.

GROWING IN DISCERNMENT

As you answer the following questions, you'll want to have your Bible in hand, as well as your copy of the book *Living in the Daze of Deception*.

1. Why is it important to exercise extreme caution when it comes to calls for unity? (See page 116 of *Living in the Daze of Deception*.)

2. List below at least four or five of the essentials of Christianity that we must agree on (see pages 116-117):

3. On page 118 of *Living in the Daze of Deception*, an article is mentioned that calls for Muslims, Christians, and Jews to come together. What problems do you see with such a call?

4. Why does it *not* make sense to us to focus on beliefs and views we have in common and let go of our points of disagreement? (See page 119.)

5. Why do you think it would be impossible for a Christian to know spiritual unity with someone who says there are many ways to heaven?

6. What four words in 1 John 4:4 reveal the reason it's not possible for Christians to know unity with those of other faiths? (See page 120.)

7. Why is there naturally a rift between those who are of the world and those who are of God? (See page 123.)

8. What exhortation does the apostle Paul give us in 2 Corinthians 6:14? And how does he cement his argument in verses 14-16? (See pages 123-125.)

9. Does the command to not be unequally yoked mean we cannot interact at all with unbelievers? Explain. (See page 125.)

10. Why is it impossible for there to be true fellowship or agreement between believers and unbelievers? (See pages 125-126.)

11. What is the clear dividing line between the sons of God and the sons of disobedience? (See pages 126-127.)

12. For those who are born of God, what does true unity arise from? (See page 127.)

13. Study the chart on pages 127-128 of *Living in the Daze of Deception*, and answer the following:

    a. Which two or three contrasts stand out to you most, and why?

    b. Which one or two of these differences have you experienced most recently in your interactions with unbelievers? What happened?

c. The chart says that believers rally around the Bible—that is, the Bible is their authority in everything they do. But for unbelievers, that is not the case. Why do you think this makes unity particularly difficult?

14. What does Ephesians 4:1-6 feature as the centerpiece of true unity? (See page 129.)

15. What Christlike attitudes are essential to experiencing unity in the body of Christ? (See page 130.)

16. Name and describe the one important quality that sets Christian unity apart from other kinds of unity. (See page 130.)

SEEKING CLARITY

"Can you say today that you are wholly committed to a faith that rests solely and wholly upon the biblical truths regarding the risen Lord, Jesus Christ? I pray it is so, for Christ alone is the cornerstone of true Christian unity."

Living in the Daze of Deception, page 130

17. When it comes to unity, in what ways would compromise make our lives *easier*?

18. And in what ways would compromise make our lives *more difficult*?

19. In what ways do you think compromise would affect our relationship with God and our usefulness to Him?

LIVING WISELY

20. Compromise is so widespread in today's culture that, much of the time, we don't notice it. What principles can you find in the following passages that can help you to grow in your ability to be discerning?

    a. Proverbs 4:23—

    b. Ephesians 5:8-10—

c. 2 Timothy 2:15—

d. James 1:5—

e. 1 John 2:15—

21. Though Scripture warns us not to be unequally yoked in partnerships or fellowship with unbelievers (2 Corinthians 6:14), that doesn't mean shutting them out of our lives. We're to show Christian love to unbelievers just as Christ did. We're called to be salt and light to the lost (Matthew 5:13-16). That means building bridges that lead to opportunities to interact and communicate with them. It means being available, especially in times of need.

What are some constructive ways we can interact with unbelievers without compromising our convictions?

PRAYING DILIGENTLY

Ask God to help you grow in discernment so that you are able to recognize compromise and avoid it. Seek to become an ambassador for Christ who takes an uncompromising stand for truth and, at the same time, reaches out to others in compassion and love.

DAZED BY THE DECEPTION
OF NEW TOLERANCE

We live in a world where words are being redefined to accommodate the whims of a culture that has strayed far from truth. In fact, there are many who say there is no "one truth" that we must all agree upon. They say truth is relative, and that what may be true for one person won't necessarily be true for another.

One word that has been maligned by revisionists is the word *tolerance*. At one time, people clearly understood that to be tolerant of someone was to be gracious to them even though we disagreed with them. To be tolerant was to be willing to let others express divergent views. It was fine to agree to disagree and be civil about it.

But now, we are told we must agree with and embrace those whom we disagree with. We're told that to merely express an opposing opinion—no matter how kindly we do so—is to be hateful and intolerant.

Not only that, but the "rules" about tolerance keep changing. It is secular culture that gets to redefine the meaning of the term. And we who are Christians are expected to go along. If we don't, then we are told we're unloving and bigoted.

You have likely experienced the redefinition of words in other ways. *Abortion* has been replaced with *reproductive health care*. *Love* has taken on shades of meaning that make unbiblical kinds of sex socially acceptable. On the surface, the term *social justice* may sound innocent, but in today's culture, the meaning behind it is far removed from true, biblical justice. And there are many words we're told not to use altogether because they can be interpreted wrongly and trigger negative emotions in people.

Ultimately, the purpose behind the redefinition of words or cancelling them is to advance hidden agendas. Frequently, these agendas run contrary to biblical truth or values, and they are manipulative and deceiving. This forces us to be more alert than ever to what we read and hear.

The area in which we are seeing some of the greatest damage occur today is related to the new tolerance, which deceives people on multiple fronts. Let's learn what we can about the new tolerance, and why it's so dangerous.

GROWING IN DISCERNMENT

As you answer the following questions, you'll want to have your Bible in hand, as well as your copy of the book *Living in the Daze of Deception*.

1. What do Webster's definitions of *tolerance* and *tolerate* mean? (See page 132 of *Living in the Daze of Deception*.)

2. What has been the traditional understanding of the virtue of tolerance? (See page 132.)

3. Today, we're told that to disagree with someone—no matter how nicely—is intolerant. What error do you see in that logic?

4. What has been the end result of the newly defined tolerance? (See page 133.)

5. What does our culture say to Christians who share the gospel or Christian beliefs? (See page 134.)

6. What does today's culture say individuals are entitled to, and how are we expected to respond? (See page 134.)

7. Under the new tolerance, right and wrong are open for interpretation. What kind of reasoning or excuses are people now using to justify wrong? (See page 136.)

8. Isaiah 5:20 says, "Woe to those who call evil good, and good evil." In what ways have you recently seen evil called good, or good called evil?

9. The new tolerance demands that Christians "stay within...prescribed boundaries." How is this actually a form of intolerance, and how is it affecting the church? (See page 138.)

10. Romans 13:1-7 clearly calls for Christians to obey the governing leaders. But what is the one exception, according to Acts 5:28-29? (See page 139.)

11. We're told that to hold to the Bible's moral standards makes us intolerant. But why is it actually loving for us to speak out against sin? (See page 141.)

12. Unbelievers may claim God is intolerant. But what does Romans 2:4 reveal? (See page 142.)

13. Why should we be willing to bear with the intolerance others express toward us? (See page 142.)

14. What does Scripture urge us to do toward our enemies, according to Romans 12:20-21? (See page 143.)

15. On page 144 of *Living in the Daze of Deception*, we read, "Whenever believers allow themselves to be guided by the feelings of unbelievers, they're right where Satan wants them: fearful of speaking the truth." What are two or three examples of truths that Christians are often afraid to say?

16. What does combatting the rising tide of the new tolerance require? (See pages 144-145.)

17. We grow spiritually stronger every time we do what? (See page 145.)

SEEKING CLARITY

"Believer, tolerance, in its truest sense, is not for the faint of heart. The Lord knows that you and I live in a world filled with hostility and anger. It would be great if, as soon as we were born again, we went straight to heaven. But by the decree of God, we remain in this world...

"God has asked us to go out into the unbelieving world and be around those who commit...sins. Don't build yourself a Christian fortress and hide there. Go with wisdom and understanding to influence the world for the glory of God. Go to those who are hurting and love them without assimilating their beliefs. This is what it means to be in the world but not of it."

Living in the Daze of Deception, page 144

18. In John 17, Jesus prayed to the Father, making this request on behalf of all believers: "I do not pray that You should take them out of the world, but that You should keep them from the evil one. They are not of the world, just as I am not of the world" (verses 15-16). God has a purpose for us *in* this world, but we are not to be *of* the world.

Looking to Jesus as a role model, how did He minister *in* the world without being *of* it? Give three examples:

a. Example 1:

b. Example 2:

c. Example 3:

19. In what ways does looking to Jesus' example help you?

LIVING WISELY

20. We've looked at Romans 12:2 earlier, but let's look at it again with the peer pressure of the new tolerance in mind. The new tolerance is working overtime to reshape our views and get us to let go of our convictions. Yet Romans 12:2 says, "Do not be conformed to this world, but be transformed by the renewing of your mind." In other words, rather than letting the world influence us, we should influence the world.

Below, list three ways you've noticed the world is trying to reshape your thinking.

  a. Pressure point 1:

  b. Pressure point 2:

  c. Pressure point 3:

21. Now, with the help of the truths and principles found in God's Word, list ways that you can respond to those pressure points biblically. If you need help, use a Bible dictionary or concordance.

  a. Biblical response 1:

  b. Biblical response 2:

c. Biblical response 3:

PRAYING DILIGENTLY

It's not easy to be the target of an intolerant world and respond with the same kind of tolerance that God exhibits—to be gracious, loving, and forgiving. Ask the Lord to fill your heart with patience and compassion for unbelievers, and to help you endure their intolerance in the hopes that they will recognize their need for God. Pray that "your light so shine[s] before men, that they may see your good works and glorify your Father in heaven" (Matthew 5:16).

DAZED BY THE DECEPTION OF THE WORLD

The world we live in is filled with bad actors who are determined to do whatever it takes to implement their agendas. To accomplish their goals, it's necessary for them to exercise greater control over how things are done. And that, in turn, means diminishing the different freedoms people have—including religious freedom.

The elite progressives who want to advance their agendas see various freedoms as a hindrance to achieving their objectives. That is why they are such big advocates of government control. And they know one effective way to increase government authority is through crises. They know that when an emergency occurs, it's easier to impose new regulations that are supposedly for the good of all, but in reality, give governing authorities more power and coerce people into submission.

Manipulation and deception are two very effective tools in the hands of global bad actors and their institutions. That is why it is so necessary for us to be extra cautious about accepting anything we read or hear. Only when we are well informed can we exercise discernment and determine what can or cannot be trusted.

The Christian values that have long helped the Western world to distinguish between good and evil are now being erased by progressives who want to replace them with the values they want everyone to adopt. These bad actors don't want freedom of thought—they don't want people to think for themselves. Instead, they want total conformity to their way of thinking.

It's vital that we learn how to recognize how all this is being done. On the surface, it appears that global elitists have everyone's best interest in mind. But they don't. Let's find out what we need to watch for.

GROWING IN DISCERNMENT

As you answer the following questions, you'll want to have your Bible in hand, as well as your copy of the book *Living in the Daze of Deception*.

1. What is one of the tactics of deception? (See page 148 of *Living in the Daze of Deception*.)

2. When it comes to informing ourselves, what should we ask the Holy Spirit to do? (See page 148.)

3. Why do the enemies of freedom want to silence certain voices? (See pages 148-149.)

4. Why do authoritarian leaders want to tamper with history? (See page 149.)

5. What does eliminating true accounts of the past accomplish for authoritarian governments? (See page 149.)

6. Once someone controls what is known about history, what else becomes easier to control? (See page 149.)

7. What point did Jonathan Swift make in the 1710 article quoted on page 150 of *Living in the Daze of Deception*?

8. During the world's confusing experience with COVID, what was the intent of the deception and manipulation? (See page 152.)

9. What are activists able to accomplish by using the word *crisis* rather than *change*? (See page 152.)

10. When it comes to climate change issues, what are activists worshipping and serving? (See page 155.)

11. What is the World Economic Forum? (See page 156.)

12. What did Klaus Schwab say in his call for a Great Reset, and what is the goal of this reset? (See page 156.)

13. What is one of the visions of the World Economic Forum with regard to restructured cities? (See pages 157-158.)

14. Why is it seemingly odd for the World Economic Forum to welcome China so warmly? (See page 159.)

15. The World Economic Forum says we have entered a phase of "permacrisis." What is meant by this? (See page 160.)

16. What tactic did Stonewall Jackson use to deceive the Union army, and similarly, what do today's global elites want us to believe? (See pages 161-162.)

17. Why should we not worry about today's massive wave of deception? (See page 162.)

SEEKING CLARITY

"Because of the Lord Jesus Christ, we know how the story ends—He will prevail!"
Living in the Daze of Deception, page 162

18. Human governments will always have agendas that are self-serving. And any government that doesn't look to God as the ultimate authority in all matters of life is sure to stray from God's ideals. It is because governments refuse to acknowledge God that the culture ends up in a downward trajectory that calls good evil, and calls evil good (see Isaiah 5:20).

But Psalm 37:13 tells us that God will have the last laugh. No one will escape His judgment. What do the following passages tell us about the battle between human authority and God's authority?

a. Proverbs 19:21—

b. Proverbs 21:1—

c. Isaiah 46:9-10—

d. Daniel 2:21—

e. Daniel 4:35—

19. Read 1 Chronicles 29:11-12. These words were spoken by King David, a human authority who recognized God as ruler over all. What truths in these verses stand out to you most, and why?

LIVING WISELY

20. All through history, human governments have failed, one after another. Their mistakes serve as a lesson that it never pays to ignore God's authority.

    Scripture is filled with reminders of the blessings and benefits of yielding ourselves fully to the Lord. What do the following passages have to say about the value and rewards of seeking God and obeying Him?

    a. Proverbs 3:5-6—

    b. Matthew 6:33—

    c. Romans 12:1-2—

    d. James 4:7-10—

    e. 1 Peter 5:6—

21. Can you think of two or three examples of blessings you've experienced that confirm the benefit of yielding to God's authority? Share them here.

22. Even though unbelievers do not submit to God, why do you think it is good for them to see your obedience to God? What positive effect could your example of submission have on them?

PRAYING DILIGENTLY

Ask God to enable you, with the Holy Spirit's help, to be cautious and discerning about everything you read and hear. Ask especially for the wisdom needed to fulfill your obligations as a citizen of earth as well as heaven—that you would glorify Christ in your submission to the government, as commanded in Romans 13:1-7, and that you would respond biblically in the times when the laws of the land directly violate the Word of God (Acts 5:28-29). Commit yourself to being consistent in your obedience to the Lord so that you may be "blameless and harmless, children of God without fault in the midst of a crooked and perverse generation, among whom you shine as lights in the world" (Philippians 2:15).

DAZED BY THE ULTIMATE DECEIVER

B ack in the days of Noah, the fog of deception was thick. Sin was raging out of control. Genesis 6:5 tells us just how bad things were: "The wickedness of man was great in the earth, and... every intent of the thoughts of his heart was only evil." Those last two words—"only evil"—paint a grim scene. Mankind was so utterly corrupt that conditions couldn't get worse. The world was so far gone that judgment was the only answer.

God commanded Noah to build an ark, and only eight people were spared from His wrath when the floodwaters came: Noah, his wife, and their three sons and their wives.

The Bible warns us we are approaching a day when evil will be just as bad again. When the disciples asked Jesus about the sign of His coming, the Lord said that before His return, it will be "as the days of Noah" (Matthew 23:37). That's the direction our world is headed, and the darkness is already overwhelming right now.

The daze is getting thicker, and people are abandoning and rejecting God. All of this is setting the stage for the rise of the Antichrist, who will be the ultimate deceiver.

One reason we can safely say the Antichrist will be the worse deceiver ever is because Scripture tells us he will be a puppet controlled by Satan himself. Revelation 13:4 tells us that the dragon, or Satan, will give authority to the beast, or the Antichrist. In 2 Thessalonians 2:8, the apostle Paul called the Antichrist "the lawless one." He then said that "the coming of the lawless one is according to the working of Satan" (verse 9). Satan will empower and direct the Antichrist.

We also know that the Antichrist will rule the world—he will have "authority...over every tribe, tongue, and nation" (Revelation 13:7). Because he is "the man of sin," "the son of perdition," and "the lawless one" (2 Thessalonians 2:3, 8), we can be sure he will do all he can to unleash unprecedented levels of sin and evil upon the entire world.

Earth's darkest days are still ahead. The daze will get worse than we can ever imagine. Let's see what we can learn about the ultimate deceiver.

GROWING IN DISCERNMENT

As you answer the following questions, you'll want to have your Bible in hand, as well as your copy of the book *Living in the Daze of Deception*.

1. Read Judges 17:6. What were people like in the days of the judges?

2. What warning did Jesus give in Luke 21:28-31? (See page 164 of *Living in the Daze of Deception*.)

3. Even though today's Christians will never see the Antichrist because the rapture will remove us from earth before he rises, what are three reasons to know about him? (See pages 164-165.)

   a. Reason 1:

   b. Reason 2:

   c. Reason 3:

4. What does the term *antichrist* mean? (See page 165.)

5. What does Paul deal with in 1 Thessalonians? (See page 165.)

6. What about 2 Thessalonians? (See page 165.)

7. Because Satan doesn't know God's timeline for the last days, what does this require Satan to do? And how far back does this go? (See page 167.)

8. What does the term *Babylon* refer to, and what can be traced back to the ancient Babylonian worship system? (See page 168.)

9. Who will the Antichrist be possessed by? (See page 169.)

10. Who will be the Antichrist's assistant, and what will he do? (See page 169.)

11. Who are the three members of the unholy trinity? (See page 169.)

12. What details do we learn about the Antichrist in…

    a. Daniel 8:9?

    b. Daniel 8:25?

    c. Daniel 11:21?

13. Paying attention to the word "craft," according to Daniel 8:25, how will the Antichrist secure peace between Israel and its neighbors? (See pages 171-172.)

14. What additional details are given to us about the peace treaty mentioned in Daniel 9:27? (See page 172.)

15. How will the Antichrist exercise control over the world's population, according to Revelation 13:16? (See page 173.)

16. Why will people want to sign up for the Antichrist's identifying mark? (See page 174.)

17. Read Revelation 20:4. According to this passage, who *won't* take the mark, and what will be the consequence of their refusal? (See pages 174-175.)

18. Ultimately, there are only two forms of religious worship. What are they? (See page 176.)

19. Why will the Babylon of the end times be called a whore, and what will be the foundation of her harlotry? (See pages 176-177.)

20. What has Satan desired from the beginning? (See page 177.)

21. List below six ways we can ensure we are pure, healthy worshippers of God (see page 178):

    (1)

    (2)

    (3)

    (4)

    (5)

    (6)

SEEKING CLARITY

> "Our responsibility is to acknowledge and understand the war being waged against our soul—the place decisions are made. All the deceptions outlined in this book require a decision—accept or reject, yield or resist, allow or deny. These decisions come down to one fundamental question: To whom will I bow my knee?"
>
> *Living in the Daze of Deception*, page 179

22. When it comes to the war being waged against our soul, what two choices are before us, according to the following passages, and what are the results of those choices?

   a. Matthew 7:24-27—

   b. Galatians 5:16-23—

   c. Ephesians 4:22-24—

   d. Titus 2:11-12—

23. What are some ways you can "bow your knee" in reverence to Christ through your everyday words, attitudes, and actions?

LIVING WISELY

24. As those who have been purchased by Christ and given the guarantee of eternal life, do we have any reason to fear what Satan is able to do? What truths can we cling to in the following passages—truths meant to give us confidence and courage?

   a. James 4:7—

   b. 1 John 4:4—

   c. Jude 24—

25. Some Christians are more preoccupied with the future rise of the Antichrist than they are with the promises of the rapture and Christ's second coming. Where do the passages on the next page call us to direct our attention?

a. Philippians 3:13-14—

b. Philippians 3:20—

c. Titus 2:13—

d. Hebrews 12:1-2—

26. With regard to everyday living and the future, why is it so beneficial for us to keep our constant focus on Christ and His promises to us?

PRAYING DILIGENTLY

Ask the Lord to help you be discerning about deception, but not afraid of it. Acknowledge the fact that He who is in you is greater than he who is in the world, and commit yourself to bowing your knee at all times to the Lord. Rejoice that Christ has already won victory over sin and Satan, and that our struggles and afflictions are temporary and our future in God's presence is certain and will last for eternity.

PART 2

STANDING FOR GOD'S TRUTH

EQUIPPED FOR LIVING IN THE LAST DAYS, PART I

The level of fear in our world today is unprecedented. Crises are affecting people more deeply than ever. The recent COVID pandemic had a far-reaching impact on everyone. It not only caused widespread panic but led to government overreach and diminished freedoms. We'll never go back to the way things were. We have all entered uncharted territory.

One of the lingering effects of the pandemic is that people have become increasingly sensitive to disasters. They are on edge because no one knows what might happen next. Since COVID, wars and other cataclysmic events have broken out. Uncertainty is everywhere, and people have no idea what tomorrow will bring. Many are finding themselves trapped in a downward spiral of despair, anxiety, and hopelessness.

But those of us who are Christians have been given a glimpse of what will happen in the future, and we know there's no reason to be afraid. God has revealed that good, righteousness, and justice will prevail. At first, evil will get worse—*far* worse—and we're seeing that happen now. Scripture tells us we are headed toward the last days, when evil will grow rampant. As we learned earlier, Jesus said the days of Noah will come back—a time in which people were "only evil continually" (Genesis 6:5). That's what is ahead of us.

Thankfully, God has not left us to figure out, on our own, how to survive the encroaching darkness and deception. He didn't say, "Hang in there—hold on as long as you can." No, God has equipped us to stand strong and be courageous. He has provided the resources we need to endure. And He will stay with us the whole way.

That is the focus of this lesson and the next: learning how to use the spiritual armament God has given us. You will be amazed at what He has provided!

GROWING IN DISCERNMENT

As you answer the following questions, you'll want to have your Bible in hand, as well as your copy of the book *Living in the Daze of Deception*.

1. What have been some of the long-term consequences of the coronavirus pandemic? (See page 183 of *Living in the Daze of Deception*.)

2. What two facts are always the same about the battles in the Old Testament? (See page 184.)

3. What valuable insight does 2 Corinthians 10:4-5 give about the warfare we engage in? (See page 184.)

4. Why are we urged to "put on the whole armor of God"? (See page 185.)

5. Whose strength do we fight in, according to the phrase "be strong in the Lord and the power of His might"? (See page 186.)

6. What goes through your mind upon reading that "the night is far spent, the day is at hand. Therefore let us cast off the works of darkness, and let us put on the armor of light" (Romans 12:12)?

7. What manner of people are we urged to be, according to Romans 12:13-14? (See page 186.)

8. What does Ephesians 6:11-12 warn that we are up against? (See page 188.)

9. What was Satan's goal when he sifted Peter? And what did God do instead? (See page 189.)

10. On page 190 of *Living in the Daze of Deception*, we read, "Faith sees what fear cannot." Can you share an example, from your own life, of a time when faith saw something that fear could not?

11. What is one method of countering spiritual attacks? (See page 191.)

12. Why is girding ourselves with God's truth so important? (See pages 192.)

13. From a practical perspective, how does God's Word help us, according to Psalm 119:105? (See page 194.)

14. The Puritans believed there were two aspects to the church: the church militant and the church triumphant.

    a. What is meant by the church militant? (See page 195.)

    b. What is meant by the church triumphant? (See page 196.)

15. In what way did Jesus pray for us in John 17:16-19? (See page 196.)

16. Why can we go forth with great courage? (See page 196.)

17. What are the eyes of the Lord looking for? (See page 196.)

18. How does 2 Corinthians 6:7 say we are to serve God? (See page 196.)

SEEKING CLARITY

"The entire Bible lays down truths we should know—line upon line, precept upon precept. Our responsibility is to follow the example of the Berean believers in Acts 17:11. They searched the Scriptures daily to determine whether the teachings they were hearing lined up with Old Testament prophecies and doctrines. And for that there is no substitute but to consume the Bible on a regular basis and determine to put it into practice."

Living in the Daze of Deception, page 194

19. God's Word has incredible power. His truth is our source of wisdom and strength as we navigate the hazards of a world filled with deception. What are some of the many ways Scripture is able to help us?

    a. Psalm 19:7-11—

    b. 2 Timothy 3:16-17—

    c. Hebrews 4:12—

20. On page 194 of *Living in the Daze of Deception*, we read, "When you walk in the truth of God's Word, it illuminates everything around you that is shadowy and distorted." What are some ways that, in recent months, the Bible has given you specific direction or clarity that you needed?

LIVING WISELY

21. On pages 194-195 of *Living in the Daze of Deception*, we read, "God has been preparing His church and is calling us to a new level of even greater commitment. He has appointed each of us to be alive at this moment in time." Consider your current life circumstances. You have a realm of influence that no one else has. What are some ways God can use you because of where He has planted you?

22. Think of a circumstance, issue, or problem you are facing right now. In what ways can God's Word illuminate your path and give you direction? What godly role models or which passages in Scripture would be helpful for you to study and learn from? Using Scripture, figure out the advice or guidance you need, and put it into action.

PRAYING DILIGENTLY

Ask the Lord to give you a deep and never-ending thirst for His Word. Acknowledge that the truths found in Scripture are your front line of protection in the daze that surrounds you. Thank God for the wisdom, direction, comfort, and hope that are yours as you read the Bible and let it dwell in you richly. Ask God to help you be faithful in consuming His Word and living it out.

EQUIPPED FOR LIVING IN THE LAST DAYS, PART 2

How often have you found yourself baffled because people so easily believe lies even when the truth is obvious?

The fact there are so many who are gullible to today's lies reveals the sad state of our world today. People will listen only to what they want to hear. The apostle Paul warned about this when he wrote, "The time will come when they will not endure sound doctrine, but according to their own desires, because they have itching ears, they will heap up for themselves teachers; and they will turn their ears away from the truth, and be turned aside to fables" (2 Timothy 4:3-4).

We are living in that time right now. People have lost the ability to exercise judgment or use logic. They are unable to tell the difference between truth and error, right and wrong. As Paul said, "according to their own desires," they will reject truth, and embrace fables.

This puts us as Christians in a difficult position. Truths that seem obvious to us won't be obvious to others. We're up against a world that says, "You have your truth, I have my truth. Everyone has their own truth." When we try to point out that two "truths" that contradict one another cannot possibly both be true, we're told that we're bigoted and hateful.

In the face of such opposition, it's easy to get discouraged or give up. That's exactly what the adversary wants. The less resistance he faces, the more successful he will be. But Scripture tells us that's not the answer. God has given us resources that enable us to stand strong in the middle of the spiritual warfare that's raging all around us. When we stand for truth and proclaim it, we shine God's light into the darkness, and we give the opportunity for those who have been blinded by the daze of deception to find their way to God.

God doesn't call us to be bold without giving us the ability to protect ourselves from Satan's fiery darts. We've been given a spiritual armor that is effective because it is backed by God's own power. And with God as our commander—the same God who *already* defeated Satan at the cross—we can engage effectively in spiritual battle at this time when our influence is needed most.

GROWING IN DISCERNMENT

As you answer the following questions, you'll want to have your Bible in hand, as well as your copy of the book *Living in the Daze of Deception.*

1. What encouraging truths does God communicate to us in Jeremiah 29:11-13? (See page 198.)

2. What promises did God make to Joshua in Joshua 1:5-7—and by extension, to everyone who honors God by obeying His commands? (See pages 198-199.)

3. With regard to our spiritual armor—what happens when we accept Christ's blood-bought payment for our sins? (See page 200.)

4. What is significant about the placement of the breastplate—that is, what does it cover? (See page 200.)

5. According to Proverbs 28:1, how does righteousness help us? (See page 200.)

6. One aspect of our armor is having our feet shod with "the gospel of peace" (Ephesians 6:15). When we wear our complete armor, we will share the gospel. Is there any legitimate excuse for a believer to not share the gospel? Explain. (See pages 201-202.)

7. What does Ephesians 6:16 say is the purpose of the "shield of faith"? (See page 203.)

8. Why can we legitimately say that our faith—as it rests in the power and truth of the Bible—is our greatest possession? (See page 204.)

9. Why is it so vital for Christians to be strongly linked together? (See 1 Peter 5:8 and pages 204-205.)

10. What does the "helmet of salvation" (Ephesians 6:17) help defend us against? (See page 205.)

11. One reason many Christians are vulnerable in spiritual battle is because they don't fully understand the nature and security of their salvation. What great truths about salvation do we find in...

     a. Romans 10:9? (see page 205)

     b. John 10:28-29? (see pages 205-206)

     c. 2 Corinthians 1:21-22? (see page 206)

12. Why do you think it is so essential for us to remember, at all times, that absolutely nothing can separate us from God's love? (See pages 206-207.)

13. What great truth does Romans 8:37 declare about those who belong to Christ? (See page 207.)

14. In what way is the "sword of the Spirit" (Ephesians 6:17) different from all the other weapons we have? (See page 107.)

15. What observation did William Gurnall make about the Word of God? (See page 208.)

16. Why is it vital that we handle God's Word skillfully in today's world? (See page 208.)

17. What does prayer do to all the other parts of our spiritual armor? (See page 209.)

18. Why does Satan want us to feel intimidated or frustrated by prayer? (See page 209.)

19. What happens when we pray? (See pages 209-210.)

20. What is the advantage of constant prayers? (See page 210.)

21. Read 1 Peter 1:3-9 in your Bible or on pages 211-212.

    a. What has God done for us, according to verses 3-5? (See page 211.)

    b. How do trials help us, according to verses 6-9? (See pages 211-212.)

22. Why do you think every day that we wake up to something else going wrong, we have cause for increased hope? (See page 212.)

23. What should the hope of Christ's return cause us to do? (See page 212.)

SEEKING CLARITY

"As you move forward, may you be the kind of believer who causes hell to sit up and take notice as heaven applauds you and the great cloud of witnesses rejoices over your faithfulness to the Lord Jesus Christ."

Living in the Daze of Deception, page 213

24. Read Ephesians 6:10-18 carefully, and answer the following questions:

    a. What pieces of our spiritual armor stand out to you, and why?

    b. Why does it make sense that the "sword of the Spirit"—that is, the Word of God—is the only offensive weapon we are given, while all the others are defensive?

    c. What does the fact we are to be "praying always with all prayer and supplication" (Ephesians 6:18) tell you about the value of prayer?

25. Read the following passages. What attitudes and perspectives are we called to have when it comes to living the Christian life, which includes engaging in spiritual warfare?

    a. Philippians 3:13-14—

b. 2 Timothy 2:3-4—

c. Hebrews 12:1-2—

LIVING WISELY

26. Do you begin each day by proactively asking God for His protection and help for the battles you face? What advantages are there to taking the time to (1) identify our battles, (2) yield them to the Lord, and (3) make sure we are relying on the spiritual armor He has given us?

27. Below, write the top three or four ways you have been helped by the *Living in the Daze of Deception* book and workbook. What have you learned that will help you to navigate the fog of deception with greater wisdom, confidence, and courage?

PRAYING DILIGENTLY

Thank the Lord for His promises that He will strengthen you, help you, and uphold you in His righteous right hand (Isaiah 41:10), and that He will stay with you wherever you go (Joshua 1:9). Thank Him for the spiritual armor He has given you and commit to being intentional about using it. Whenever fear strikes, don't let it paralyze you. Go to the Lord immediately and ask Him to give you courage and peace. Place your full trust in His promise to be faithful and supply you with everything you need to fulfill His calling for your life.